TELL ME WHY™

We Need the Amazon Rain Forest

illustrated by

ROBERT E. WELLS   PATRICK CORRIGAN

Albert Whitman & Company
Chicago, Illinois

For Kim, Mike, Rowan, Annalise, Aria, and Corin—REW

To my friends and family—PC

Library of Congress Cataloging-in-Publication data is on file with the publisher.
Text copyright © 2023 by Robert E. Wells
Illustrations copyright © 2023 by Albert Whitman & Company
Illustrations by Patrick Corrigan
First published in the United States of America in 2023 by Albert Whitman & Company
ISBN 978-0-8075-7780-6 (hardcover) • ISBN 978-0-8075-7781-3 (ebook)
Printed in China
10 9 8 7 6 5 4 3 2 1 WKT 28 27 26 25 24 23
Design by Shane Tolentino
For more information about Albert Whitman & Company, please visit our website at www.albertwhitman.com.

If you have plans to play outside, a rainy day might spoil your fun.

But a rainy day is a very good day for a tree.

When it rains, the water dissolves minerals in the soil. Minerals are the substances that make up Earth's soil, sand, and rocks. This water-and-mineral mixture is absorbed by a tree's roots and travels up the trunk through long thin tubes to the leaves and branches, giving the tree nourishment, or food, to grow.

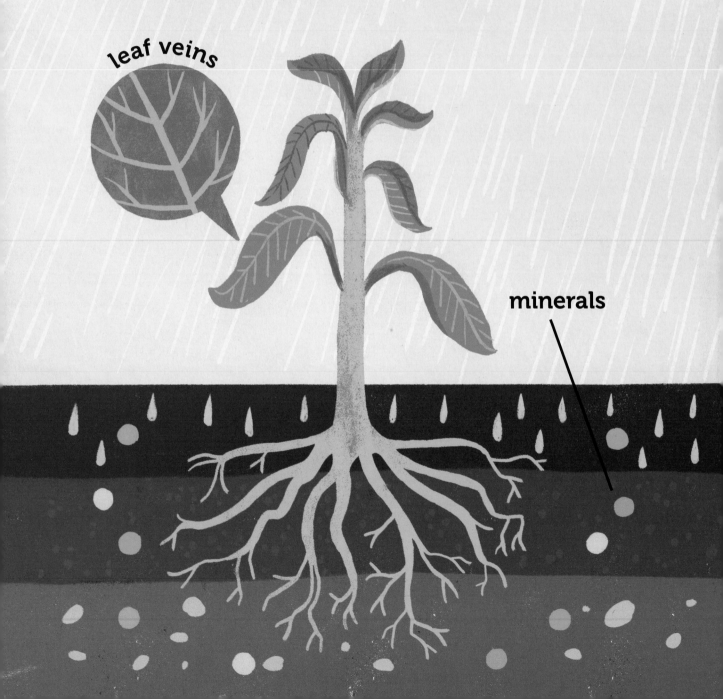

leaf veins

minerals

When a great number of trees grow in the same area, it's called a forest. Forests grow on every continent, or large land mass, on Earth—except Antarctica, where it is too cold and icy. And all those trees need water.

As you can probably tell from their name, rain forests get more rain than any other kind of forest. There are two kinds of rain forests: temperate and tropical. Temperate rain forests grow near coasts, where the climate is cooler. Tropical rain forests grow on or near the equator, where it is hot and wet. The Amazon rain forest in South America is Earth's biggest tropical rain forest.

temperate
rain forest

Rain forests are the world's oldest ecosystems, which are communities of all the living and nonliving things in an area, interacting with their environment. Rain forests are home to more than half the world's plants and animals, even though they cover less than 10 percent of Earth's land.

tropical rain forest

Imagine all the birds, animals, flowers and butterflies that live in the Amazon rain forest. It covers about 2,000,000 square miles. That's more than half the size of the United States.

But visiting there would be even better.
It's a perfect time for a family adventure!

You'll need a good guide and a place to stay. Your travel book recommends Alfonzo's River Tours. Alfonzo also owns a hotel near the forest.

Your trip is set! Reservations have been made, backpacks are ready, and your neighbor Mr. Sanders is glad to water your plants while you're on your great adventure.

As planned, Alfonzo meets you at the airport with his spider monkey, Spiro. Your family is delighted to have a real spider monkey as an extra tour guide!

After a night's rest, your forest tour begins. The Amazon River flows along the forest floor, where many animals eat, play, and sleep. As you float along the river in the early morning, the dark forest is filled with a chorus of sound—chirping crickets, singing birds, and croaking frogs.

But suddenly, the peaceful sounds of the forest are shattered by a deafening roar. It is the shriek of a howler monkey, who can roar even louder than a lion.

There are four layers, or levels, in a rain forest.
Emergent trees form the highest layer, stretching
their branches about 200 feet into the sky.

The next layer, standing about 100 feet high,
is made up of canopy trees.

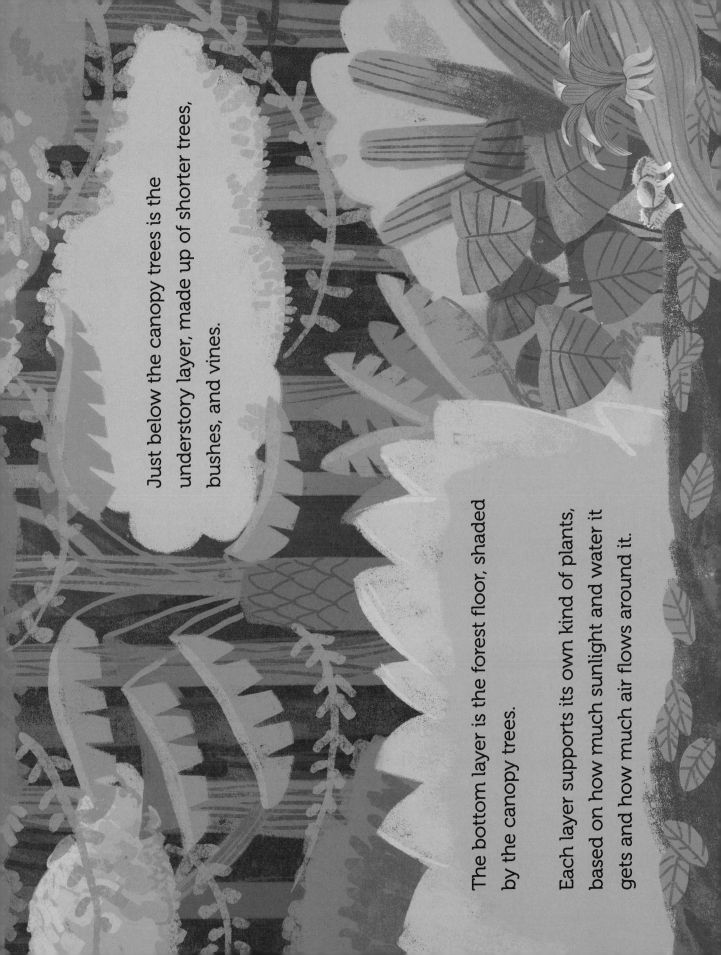

Just below the canopy trees is the understory layer, made up of shorter trees, bushes, and vines.

The bottom layer is the forest floor, shaded by the canopy trees.

Each layer supports its own kind of plants, based on how much sunlight and water it gets and how much air flows around it.

The Amazon River is quieter than the forest surrounding it but just as full of life.

Swimming in the river below your boat are some of the thousands of species of fish that supply food for people who live in the forest. The fish also provide income for families who sell them.

Acrobatic animals swing in the branches and vines of the canopy trees. The star acrobats are the spider monkeys. They have prehensile tails, that, like an extra hand, can grip branches and vines to help them move from tree to tree.

Squirrel monkeys like to climb the tall emergent trees and eat berries and nuts from epiphytes, plants that grow on rain forest trees.

But when a harpy eagle descends suddenly from the sky, searching the treetops for prey, the monkeys—like all the other animals high in the trees—must quickly retreat to the forest floor below to avoid being eaten.

It rains nearly every day in the Amazon. Sometimes the rain falls in thundering cloudbursts, crashing wildly on the canopy trees below.

The heavy rain is slowed by the dense canopy leaves and drips slowly to the forest floor without washing away the forest soil.

The Amazon rain forest is very important for life on Earth. Its billions of trees and plants produce much of the oxygen all living things need—so much oxygen that the Amazon is sometimes called "the lungs of the world."

When rain falls on land that has been cleared of trees, there are fewer tree roots to hold the soil in place and no canopy trees to slow the heavy rainfall. Much of the top layer of soil is washed away. The remaining soil is low in the nutrients that would nourish any crops that farmers would choose to grow. Because the land is no longer good for farming, it is soon abandoned.

The world needs rain forests, but the Amazon rain forest is in danger of being destroyed. Too much forestland has been cleared to be used for growing crops and raising cattle, and too many trees have been cut down and sold for lumber so people can build houses and furniture.

When rain forest trees are destroyed, climates are changed all over the world. Our atmosphere, the air we breathe, is made up mostly of the gases oxygen and nitrogen. But it also contains a small amount of carbon dioxide, a natural gas that can store some of the sun's heat.

Because there are so many cars, trucks and factories burning oil and coal, which all contain carbon dioxide, too much of this gas is being released into the air. Since carbon dioxide retains heat, the extra carbon dioxide has caused Earth's average temperature to rise. And now, because Earth's temperature is slowly rising, climates are changing.

The rising temperature has changed the Amazon's climate. Dry seasons are drier, causing more fires to be started by lightning—and in recent years, more fires have been set on purpose to clear forest land for farms and ranches.

Trees and plants absorb carbon dioxide and use it to grow—
the countless trees, bushes, and epiphytes in rain forests
together absorb great quantities of carbon dioxide. When trees
are destroyed, less carbon dioxide is absorbed from the air.
The burning of trees also releases the carbon dioxide that they
store, causing even more warming of the air.

The Amazon rain forest is home to millions of species of plants and animals. Its biodiversity, or the many different kinds of plants and animals living in it, cannot be replaced. Every one of the Amazon rain forest's species is important to the biodiversity of the whole world.

We need the Amazon rain forest—and the
Amazon rain forest needs us to protect it.

Glossary

Antarctica: An icy continent located around the South Pole.

canopy trees: Trees located just below those at the emergent level of a rain forest.

carbon dioxide: A heavy, colorless gas that absorbs and stores heat.

climate: The typical weather in a certain place measured over a period of time.

emergent trees: The tallest trees in a rain forest, which make up the forest's top layer.

epiphytes: Plants that grow upon other plants, taking nutrients from air and rain instead of soil.

equator: A circle around the earth that is equally distant from the North Pole and South Pole.

minerals: Solid, nonliving natural substances that are found in soil, rocks, and water.

nitrogen: An odorless, colorless gas that makes up more than three-fourths of Earth's atmosphere.

nutrients: Substances needed by living things to survive and grow.

oxygen: A gas found naturally in Earth's atmosphere that humans and other animals need to breathe.

prehensile: Able to grab onto things, such as a hand does.

Selected Sources

Cherry, Lynne. *The Great Kapok Tree: A Tale of the Amazon Rain Forest*. San Diego: Harcourt Brace Jovanovich, 1990.

Clarke, Ginjer L. *Life in the Amazon Rainforest*. New York: Penguin Young Readers, 2018.

Fabiny, Sarah. *Where is the Amazon?* New York: Grosset & Dunlap, 2016.

Krebs, Laurie. *We're Roaming in the Rainforest: An Amazon Adventure*. Cambridge, MA: Barefoot Books, 2010.

Mitchell, Susan K. *The Rainforest Grew All Around*. Mount Pleasant, SC: Sylvan Dell Publishing, 2007.

Munro, Roxie. *Anteaters, Bats & Boas: The Amazon Rainforest from the Forest Floor to the Treetops*. New York: Holiday House, 2021.